A STRATEGIC PLAN
for
Ministry

A Business Owner's Guide
to Business as Ministry

ISBN13: 978-0-9786039-4-6
ISBN: 0-9786039-4-X
For Worldwide Distribution
Printed in the U.S.A.

Lanphier Press
U.S.A.
www.lanphierpress.com

CHRISTIAN CEOS & OWNERS
BUILDING GREAT BUSINESSES
FOR A GREATER PURPOSE ™

The C12 Group, LLC
U.S.A.
www.c12group.com

Contents

Chapters

Appendices

The Field – A Parable

A man stood by the side of a field watching his laborers at work. The field was heavy with fruit, ripe and rich for harvest. The laborers worked steadily, productively.

Another appeared beside the man. "A fine field," he said.

"Yes," said the first man, "it is abundant. I am blessed".

They stood watching for awhile. Then the other said, "Workers one, three and seven are lost and do not have eternal life".

"What's that to me?" said the first man, "I am not a preacher and they have only come to me for work."

"True enough," the other replied, "They have come to you for work. But what of the matter of their souls? Have you not the gift that you received, and could you not share it with them? They respect you since you have been good and honest. Your wages are fair and you have dependably cared for them. If you speak to them, they will listen."

"I have never thought of such a thing," the first said, "I am a businessman, not a preacher. This is a business, not a church."

"If they die as they are, they will burn in hell apart from the presence of God forever," said the other, "and should that happen, those who had the chance to offer Eternal Life to them, and did not, will be guilty of indifference, and their indifference will cause them great sorrow and loss. Great opportunity, which if lost through indifference, is a very sad thing. Your opportunity is great because they will listen if you speak to them. They look to you."

"But what of my business?" the first queried, "If I take time to talk to them, they would be less fruitful in the work."

"Look," the other replied, "they are talking now of many things. What if you should walk among them? Could you not speak to them? If now they fill their heads with talk of what perishes, could you not instead share with them the way to Eternal Life?"

> For each time one who has Eternal Life offers it to one who is lost and without it, he gains for himself an eternal reward, prized in the heavenlies.

"I guess I could," said the first.

"It would be wise indeed," the other replied, "for each time one who has Eternal Life offers it to one who is lost and without it, he gains for himself an eternal reward prized in the heavenlies. A wise businessman would be a fool to pass by such a profit. The crop in the field can be lost through storm or drought. It will come and go and soon you will not even remember it.

But the fruit that endures to Eternal Life is yours forever. The crop stored in Heaven is safe and can never be lost."

"I have been blind and unseeing," the first lamented. "Is it too late? Is there yet time to redeem?"

"While they are yet with you it is not too late, but hurry. For the storm clouds gather and who knows how fast the winds will blow?"

The man looked around him and the Other had disappeared.

"For everyone to whom much is given,
from him much will be required;
and to whom much has been committed,
of him they will ask the more."
Luke 12:48b

Shining Lights

"Let your light so shine among men,
that they may see your good works
and glorify your Father in Heaven."
Matthew 5:16

This familiar Scripture verse rings out a challenge undiminished through the ages. It is taken from a passage traditionally referred to as Jesus' Sermon on the Mount. This teaching has a beauty and directness that has been appreciated and honored by Christians since the founding of Christ's Church. Every Sunday School student studies it and pastors have preached on it for two millennia.

In fact, it may have become so familiar to us that we have become numb to its deeper truth. In that spirit, we will look at a portion of The Sermon on the Mount today.

First, let's examine the often overlooked context of this famous event. The first verse of Matthew's fifth chapter says, *"And seeing the multitudes, He went up on a mountain, and when He was seated His disciples came to Him. Then He opened His mouth and taught them saying..."*

The most common impression concerning this event is that Jesus was teaching the masses. Obviously, this is not so. He delivered His Sermon on the Mount to the disciples whom He had already chosen to be His closest earthly associates, friends, and students. These men were the ones to whom the task of propagating His Word was to be given. These words exemplify some of Jesus' most intimate teaching.

Today, *we* are the inheritors of the mission given those first disciples. The words of Jesus have been passed to us and the call of our Lord is upon our lives as it was upon theirs. We have the high privilege of being called as present-day disciples, living just as they did once Jesus returned to Heaven and sent His Spirit to be with them, dwelling in them.

Just as *they* were working men whom Jesus selected from the

> *...tradesmen, tax collectors, fishermen and so on. As far as we know, none of them had been to seminary. They were not religious professionals; ...they were people like you and I.*

marketplace of the time, so are *we*. They were tradesmen, tax collectors, fishermen, and so on. As far as we know, none of them had been to seminary. They were not religious professionals like the Pharisees or Sadducees; they were 'lay' people like you and I. When Jesus returned to Heaven, they continued to live their lives on earth for a season in which they served Jesus wherever He sent them. They worked and served and, as they did, God turned the world upside down through them.

The words spoken by Jesus so long ago to our spiritual fathers have been sovereignly protected in God's Living Word. These intimate words of instruction and illumination are now being spoken by Jesus directly to you and me. In order for them to be fully operative, a couple of things need to be established in our hearts.

First, these teachings are not limited to our life in the marketplace, but they certainly include it. In the same sense, they are not limited to our life in church, but they encompass it as well. Jesus never taught a divided life. His words were, and remain, for all of life. It is truly said, "He is Lord *of* all, or He's not Lord *at* all."

Second, there are not two classes of Christians; one a full-time professional clergy, with the other being the rest of us 'part-timers'. This concept is heresy. For those under the Lordship of Christ, there is no sacred/secular divide! Perhaps no other misconception has hindered and damaged the cause of Christ in modern times as much as this sort of compartmentalization. The call of God to the pulpit or overseas missionary work is no more holy than the call of God to be the president or janitor of a company. The *position* doesn't define its holiness; it is the *call* of God on each of us that defines it. Who and for what purpose He calls is the true measure, not the mere job position or title. God has *not* called you and me to labor in the marketplace merely to provide financial support for the professional clergy. His call on our lives as His disciples and ambassadors is the same as theirs. He didn't say, "Pastors and missionaries go into all the world." He just said, "GO." His call to go into all the world (including the marketplace) and to make disciples is universal to all believers, not only those in specifically church-related or religious professions. Being His disciples is an everywhere, all the time, assignment for each of us. This is our eternal identity in Christ!

Obedience to His call will be the measure of your success and mine, not the highest job title we attain or anything else. As followers of Christ, our primary call is to look for satisfaction in our work by discovering how to bring God honor through it. As Paul reminds us, "Whatever you do, work at it with all your heart, as working for the Lord and not for men!" (Colossians 3:23-24 NIV). The only thing that changes in God's call on the life of His children is the venue in which He places them. Some are called to serve Him in the Church, others in marketplace professions, some by laboring with their hands, some to bear children, and some to teach children. But His Kingdom purpose and call for each is the same. Some He enables to become wealthy while some are called to remain poor. Rich or poor is not the telling measure. In the life to come, such distinctions will have no significance at all. Only our obedience will matter in responding faithfully *in* His call on and for our lives.

Let's pause for a minute right here. Let me ask you a sobering question that, depending on your answer, will have eternal significance to you: *"Do you really, in your heart of hearts, believe that you and your place in life are every bit as holy in God's eyes as that of your pastor or any other leader in the formal church?"* Deep down in the very core of your being, do you see yourself and your work in your business, Monday through Friday, as just as important to God as whatever goes on in your church on Sunday morning and Wednesday evening? Are they just as holy and eternally vital? Are they equally loaded with potential for producing eternal fruit?

My brothers and sisters, I can tell you that until (and unless) you see them this way, you will never be all that God has called you to be. As long as we think that somehow the work that God has given us to do is less a call and less holy than that given to the religious professionals, we will never be what God has designed us to be and the Body of Christ will suffer loss and compromise. The reason for this strong statement is that as long as we think that we are involved in *secular* work while in business and *sacred* work in the church, we will continue to believe that there are two distinct standards or value systems for living available to us: one for work and another for church. Obviously, this is at odds with a life of integrity according to God's eternal principles.

How does this relate to our subject for today, letting "our light shine before men"? In the Bible, light is used to represent God or God's truth. It contrasts with darkness, which represents the evil in the world or the false system of Satan.

> *If we think that we are involved in "secular" work while in business and "sacred" work in the church, we will continue to believe that there are two standards for living...*

Our light in this sense is our "good works."

They are to shine in the world in such a way that others will see them and give credit or glory to God. This is to be true in all areas of our lives.

When our paradigm is that of a divided *sacred/secular* world, we tend not to apply the same values in each arena. We will look for sacred things in the church setting and secular things in the world of work and pleasure. We won't seek to demonstrate the contrast between our light and the world's darkness at work because we don't see the necessity. We will tend to blend in with the darkness rather than to shine brightly in contrast to it. We may even buy into the lie that in order to succeed we *must* do so, and since our work is secular, not holy, we'll probably tell ourselves that this won't really make a negative difference.

This is, of course, in exact opposition to God's revealed truth. The truth is that our light shines brightest when the contrast is the greatest. In order for light to be noticed, it must shine in darkness. When you turn on a powerful flashlight on a sunny day, it can hardly be seen. In the dark of the night, however, it becomes a bright beacon. So it is with us. When we perform works of righteousness in church, they are good but they don't stand out as clearly as the same acts would outside the church. Remember, we said that Scripture doesn't apply only to the marketplace, but that it certainly applies there as well.

> *When we do just what Jesus would do in the same circumstances, our light shines*

Our light shines when we act or react to life in ways that contrast to the ways of the world. Jesus said that He is "the light of the world" (John 8:12). His life contrasted sharply with the lives of the Pharisees and other religious and political leaders. The things He said and did were in stark contrast to the acts of the others. His "light" shone brightly, enabling people to easily see a difference between Him and the others. They could see it in His acts and hear it in His words and it gave them pause.

For us, the marketplace provides perhaps the greatest opportunity to demonstrate the enormous difference that having Christ makes in our lives. When we act or react in ways that are consistent with His teachings and ways — in contrast to the world and its ways — our light shines. Others take notice.

Our light shines when we:

- Turn the other cheek when attacked
- Respond in kindness to our enemies (competitors)
- Give erring employees another chance, extending grace (with accountability) perhaps when the world wouldn't
- Tell others that the most important thing in our lives is Jesus Christ, not worldly success, and then...
- Live so they can see that it's true
- Go the second mile when others wouldn't
- Risk looking foolish for Christ where others dare not
- Wish genuine good to all men, with the greatest good being their salvation
- Would rather see men saved than to make a profit from them
- Keep our word in spite of the fact that it may cost us dearly to do so
- Honor all men, even those of much 'lower' place than God has called us to
- Seek the best for others even when they appear disinterested
- Speak the truth in love even when it is uncomfortable
- Don't demand the privileges that our position affords us in the eyes of the world
- Avoid taking opportunistic advantage for ourselves even when we could
- Use our money to build people, rather than using our people to build money
- Do just what Jesus would do in the same circumstances. When we do, our light shines and He lives. Jesus is still The Light. He lives as we let Him shine through our good works.

This is our spiritual heritage. We have inherited it from those first disciples who sat on that mountainside near Capernaum with Jesus. He told them to "let their light shine" and, through them, this charge during the Sermon on the Mount now comes to us as His heirs and ambassadors. *We* are among those for whom Jesus prayed, who would later come to faith in Him through the disciples' message (John 17:20).

Is our call holy? Yes, as holy as any that has ever been. You and I, as we live out each day, moment-by-moment in the marketplace, are involved in a holy calling and work which involves obediently following whomever God leads. We have not been called to the pulpit of a church, but to the 'bully pulpit' of a business. We don't prepare sermons, we prepare budgets. We don't exegete the Scriptures, we model them. We are the frontline troops. If it can't happen through us, it won't happen at all. If God's Word isn't as valid and binding on Monday as it is on Sunday, are you really viewing it as valid at all?

Is this a tough message to receive? Perhaps so. Since so many have opted not to live in *this* world with their hearts in the *next*, perhaps it seems too hard. The question shouldn't be, *is it hard*, but, *is it true*?

C12 is committed not to perpetuating mediocrity, but to striving for the greatness implicit in pursuing God's highest and best in each of our lives. This is as true in the pursuit of excellence in the ministry aspect of our business lives as it is in the purely commercial performance of the enterprise. In the eternal sense, our ministry impact is infinitely more important. As servant leaders, God calls us to 'live large' where He currently has us; casting a vision, defining 'reality' for our team, and leading by example. We have the opportunity, now, to make a difference for eternity by bringing meaning and significance to a place where many only seek a paycheck.

We start where we are and work to grow from that point. No one has arrived. We are all 'in process.' Our God-given responsibility is to press on toward the high mark of the upward call of God in Christ Jesus. Along the way, following Him and allowing ourselves and our businesses to be shaped by the Potter's purpose and principles will surely result in a thrilling and fruitful ride. May *your* light so shine among men, that they may see your good works and glorify your Father in Heaven.

CHAPTER 2

Where Does Jesus Show?

Imagine being a 'fly on the wall' or somehow being able to observe your company as an employee, customer, supplier, or competitor. What would you observe on a regular basis that would lead you to think that your company belonged to Christ and was being led by a believing manager or steward? What would you see that would distinguish your company from any other secular or non-Christ-centered business?

To help you answer this question, I ask that you participate in an exercise aimed at priming your imagination. Imagination can be a powerful tool. Unfortunately, many of us quit using it shortly after the age of nine. But let's try.

Imagine arriving at work tomorrow morning, parking your car in the usual place, getting out, and walking toward the entrance. Everything seems normal so far. But as you approach the door, you notice a figure waiting just outside. As you approach, you sense a warm and open, friendly demeanor and reception. This person is obviously a friend.

A few more steps and you recognize him. It's Jesus Christ! You start to fall down to worship Him but He puts His hand on your shoulder. "Not now," He says, "I'm not here to judge you, this is just a visit. I'd like you to show me around and explain the business to me. I'm vitally interested not only in what happens at church, but here, too. My Kingdom has no end."

In your mind's eye, imagine yourself saying, "Well, fine, Lord, let's go in." And so you do.

Imagine taking Jesus through the reception area and into the office, your personal office space, through the work areas, and through the entire physical plant. Imagine His keen observation of the way you and your team interact as you take your tour. Think about explaining to Him how and why everything is laid out the way it is. Mentally introduce Him to each person and explain their function and a little about them.

> *I'm vitally interested not only in what happens at church, but here, too.*

Sit down with Him in your office or conference room and describe to Him how each piece of the business functions from the different ways of contacting customers, to the production and delivery of the product, to billing or charging the customer and collecting payment.

Talk to Him about how people are hired, trained, evaluated, encouraged, promoted, disciplined, fired. Explain how complaints from customers, suppliers, and employees are handled.

Take Him through accounting. Show Him how bills are paid and how taxes are handled. Discuss how profits are used or distributed and who benefits from them. Show

Him the debt of the company and explain how and why the leveraging works.

As you engage in each of these areas, imagine saying to Jesus, "Lord, this is how we try to show You and Your principles in this function or action...this is how we think You would do this...Lord, we do this so we won't bring offense to Your name...Jesus, we don't do this the world's way because of what You said in Your Word."

Does this process excite and encourage you or does it cause you to break out in a cold sweat?

In reality what we are describing is a visit to a branch operation by a CEO with an inspection tour guided by his local general manager. During any such tour, your major priorities emphasis and progress against corporate business plans are demonstrated and discussed.

Having been in both positions in our careers, we know a little about how each party thinks.

The visiting owner or CEO is looking to see that the basic plans for business development and growth have been implanted and are being consistently and successfully applied. He looks for results but is acutely interested in alignment, commitment and the process, knowing that if the corporate strategy is being diligently followed, the desired results will generally follow.

On the other hand, the manager being visited is anxious to demonstrate to the owner that he is doing precisely what the owner wants and is doing a good job of execution. He knows that his future rewards or promotions are dependent on how he carries out the directions of his boss. Success is measured by how well he communicates and executes the overall strategy and plan as a part of the team.

In our businesses, this review is going on all the time. God does have a plan for our lives and it includes every aspect of them: home, work, community, social, recreation and any other area you might identify.

Further, His plan always has the same end in mind, consistently reflects the same values, and, while the environment or playing field may change, His eternal purpose never changes. That timeless purpose is to manifest the gospel of Jesus Christ. Everything that God does and allows has as its ultimate purpose to bring forward the Kingdom of God. Nothing in God's world "just happens".

In our businesses, as in every other area of our lives, we can either see this reality or miss it completely. The choice is ours and it is determined by our mind-set or paradigm.

If we see our business primarily as a tool to produce money for ourselves, our primary concerns will relate to how well it is performing in that way and we will focus our attention, decisions, and actions primarily toward that end. We will try to develop strategy and deploy our people, and assets purely toward producing monetary profits.

On the other hand, we might see our businesses as a part of God's eternal plan, specially given to us and designed to fit into an intricate and beautiful master plan to strategically contribute to bringing Christ into the world and the world to Christ. In this case, our decisions and evaluations will reflect different values and we will attempt to structure what we do to produce a different set of results.

Are these two paradigms compatible? No, not in the sense of a basic underlying motivation or purpose. Jesus said it this way, "No one can serve two Masters." We cannot serve God and money. Only one can be first. We either serve God or we serve money. Money is simply a helpful tool for our use which man invented to facilitate commerce. As a medium of exchange, money helps us to effectively operate in the marketplace in such a way that we can be good stewards and glorify God by using it wisely.

Serving God in our businesses by providing for others and promoting His Kingdom and the gospel of Jesus Christ through them, means that we utilize each and every effort and activity primarily toward that end.

If profit is our primary motivation and we detect a drain or hindrance, we act quickly to correct the situation. If we find a policy hinders profitability, we eliminate it as quickly as possible. If people aren't contributing, we take action through training, transfer or termination. We strive to see how we are performing in all areas as they relate to the goal and make necessary adjustments to ensure the health of the enterprise.

We employ essentially the same approach if our primary motivation is to promote the Kingdom of God. We will look at people, policies and practices and evaluate how they conform to our principal purpose. We will then make adjustments to refine our efforts. In lean parlance, this is referred to as the plan/do/check/adjust (PDCA) cycle.

All that's different with a company dedicated to the Lord's purpose is its ultimate Owner and His desired goals. That's why this metaphor is valid. Taking Jesus through every department and practice of our company, so He can evaluate its utility, is simply acknowledging His place and position in the plan and process.

If it really is His company and He has a plan for it and for me as its steward, shouldn't every part of it be subject to His standards and promote His purposes? Of course they should!

Therefore, it becomes vitally important to consider how each part contributes to the whole. The way we work, buy and sell, hire and fire, spend and save, pay and collect, and the processes and people we promote all tell a story regarding our primary values. Each component part reflects this reality in it's own way, and together all the parts work together to present the composite picture or culture.

Can your **customers** see Jesus in your: sales people, marketing literature, invoicing, credit and collections approach, customer service, advertising, product delivery and after-sale service?

Can your **suppliers** see Him in your: negotiations and vendor selection process, paying practices, attitudes toward them, and the value of their time and other resources?

> *Can your customers see Jesus?*
> *Can your suppliers see Jesus?*
> *Can your employees see Jesus?*

Can your **employees** see Jesus in your: selection and training, performance evaluations, company policies, approach toward discipline and rewards, encouragement of desired practices, and the people you praise?

Do your **competitors** and other business people get a clue that there is something very different about you and your company as you: compete with them, refer business to them, participate in trade associations or civic organizations with them, find it tough to recruit folks away from you, and see you serving your community?

> *Do your competitors and other business people get a clue that there is something very different about you and your company?*

All of these things, you see, serve to create and comprise our corporate culture. And our corporate culture comes out of our deepest and most fervently-held purpose and paradigm. We can *say* what we want, but what we *do* discloses the truth of our hearts.

So, what if Jesus were to be waiting at the entrance for you some morning for His tour? Are you ready? Do you have thoughtful answers for His questions concerning His primary interests? Do you have a plan centered on His values and purposes to guide you as you evaluate and develop each part of the business?

If not, now would be a great time to begin to make one. The sooner the better. Because you clearly know, that while it probably won't be tomorrow, Jesus' inspection is coming! You and I don't know just when, but it will happen when we stand face-to-face with our King.

It's sort of like the television ad slogan for the oil filter, "Pay me now or pay me later." We can begin now to try to see everything as Jesus does or wait until we stand with Him at the Bema seat on Judgment day and have Him show it all to us then. What is His will last for eternity. All else will burn up. As has been so eloquently stated: "only one life, 'twill soon be past; only what's done for Christ will last". Either way, we are going to see it. The difference is that there will be huge rewards for those who invest the time and effort to know His will and do it now. There will be equally huge losses in eternity for those, and due to those, who wait until later.

Take Jesus on a plant tour or office visit now in your mind. Show Him what you think you are doing to fit into His eternal plan for you and your company. Ask Him to show you where you're on target, off-target or 'out of the picture' completely. Do it regularly, not just today, but fairly often as you have a quiet time of fellowship and meditation with Him and His Word. Ask for a performance review and look at every piece with Him. A wise manager always tries to know his boss's priorities and does his best to meet them. A wise manager who loves his Boss delights in serving Him and seeing His plans fulfilled. May your leadership efforts glorify your father in Heaven.

1. Identify each major department and function of your business:

   - _____
   - _____
   - _____
   - _____
   - _____
   - _____

2. Identify who each department primarily relates to:

   - _____
   - _____
   - _____
   - _____
   - _____
   - _____

3. Identify other important secondary and tertiary relationships:

   - _____
   - _____
   - _____
   - _____
   - _____
   - _____

4. How is Christ involved or demonstrated in these functions, activities or relationships?

   - _____
   - _____
   - _____
   - _____
   - _____
   - _____

Your Business as a Vehicle for Ministry

Sometimes we use words and terms so frequently and casually that we become numb with regard to their real meanings. For example, consider be the words *quality* and *excellence*. These words have almost lost their meaning in the world of business because so many people have applied their own meanings and interpretation to them. The wide range of observable products and services making such claims is proof positive of differing meanings. In the automotive market, for instance, Rolls Royce and Hyundai each claim to represent the highest standards of both attributes.

In C12 we seek to avoid such confusion, especially as it applies to some very fundamental and important understandings.

One of the terms or phrases we frequently use and often discuss at great length is that our businesses are "a vehicle or platform for ministry."

Our business...Is our ministry. It is the vehicle that God has given us to apply the Good News of Jesus Christ in the unique places and with the unique people that it touches.

To lose clarity in understanding the real meaning of this phrase would bring confusion to our purpose. Such distraction needs to be avoided if we are going to be effective to the highest degree possible. Clear communication is a great asset no matter what sort of relationship or enterprise we are talking about.

Words have meaning. Understanding them correctly is essential to clear communication. Let's take a risk and define what our businesses are and what they are not. We'll talk first about what they are not. Our business is *not*:

- **the source of our livelihood**. It is the means God has chosen to supply our needs at present, but He is The Source.
- **a sign that God loves us more** than others and so has given us a way to enjoy a higher standard of living or a more pleasure-filled life than they. It is a higher responsibility to live in a higher place. "To whom much is given, from him will much be required" (Luke 12:48).
- **a means to gain status or reputation** in The Kingdom of God. Owning a business implies no special spiritual standing with God. In and of itself it is irrelevant in these terms. God calls some to be poor and some to be rich. He loves them and values them equally. "God is no respecter of persons" (Acts 10:34).
- **something that God gives to us as a burden** to bear, or as an excuse for not

spending enough time with Him, our spouse, or our children. He does not give us a business *instead of* a religious calling.

We could say more about what it's not, but let's move on. If our business is not these things, what is it? Perhaps it would help to review the meaning of a few key words.

Let's take the word ministry as in "Working 'On' My MINISTRY in God's Business."

What does the word mean to you? What is ministry? For Christians it is the bringing forth of the Gospel of Jesus Christ, the good news, in all its various forms. For C12 this is the fundamental meaning we understand and seek to apply. Ministry for Christians means applying the Gospel to the situation at hand, wherever "at hand" or "along the way" might be.

What is MINISTRY? What does that word mean to you?

So a different way of expressing the term would be to say that our business is a vehicle or platform for bringing forth or applying "the good news." A vehicle is something that we use to take us somewhere or that we utilize toward some end. A platform is a foundation or basis for action or a support upon which something is built.

Taking our definition a bit further, we would say that our business is something that we use to bring forth, support, or apply the good news. Ultimately, that is all it is...a means to an end. It supports many functions and activities, but only one purpose.

Our business, and the process of doing business, IS our ministry. It is the vehicle that God has given us to apply the good news of Jesus Christ in the unique places, and with the unique people, that it touches.

How does this work? Let me give an example.

One evening several years ago, I was settling back in my seat on a flight from somewhere in the southern U.S., I don't remember just where, to Chicago. I was dog-tired. It had been a long, rough week and all I wanted to do was to read The Wall Street Journal just enough to put me to sleep. It certainly wouldn't have taken long at that point. I just wanted to awake in Chicago and get home to my family.

As I was opening the paper, I noticed my seat partner sort of smiling a timid smile in my direction. I looked away because I really didn't want to talk to her.

She spoke first, "Are you going home?"

"Yes," I answered, not wanting to say more.

"I'm not," she said," I'm visiting my son and new grand-baby."

"That's nice."

"What do you do?"

At this point I knew my plan for sleep was on hold. I had learned that when people asked me this question I was to respond in a very specific way.

"I work for a very unusual company," I said, "it's a chemical business that is a Christian company."

"How unusual," she replied, and I sensed my plan was now off hold and down the drain!

"Yes, it is unusual. We are trying to learn, and to show, how Jesus would run a business if He were the boss." I looked at her a little closer. "Sweet looking little old lady," I thought, "I wonder what The Lord has here?"

"I haven't been to church for many years. I just didn't get anything from it," she said.

"I never got much from church either, not until I met Jesus and gave my life to Him. It's different now," I replied.

You know (or can certainly guess) the rest. Maxine Smith of Greenville, Tennessee had been to church many times, but never met the Lord of the Church. Not until that night. That night she became my friend and my sister in Christ.

She went home and shared what had happened with her husband. They started to go to church together and joy entered and filled their lives. How do I know? She wrote to me for many years. What a blessing her letters were! I read them to my Sunday school class and we all learned much from Maxine. She had some real hard times but, when the Lord got her heart, He got all of it.

"A sweet story," you might think, "but what has it to do with our study?" Simply this: if it hadn't been for the business, I wouldn't have been on that plane at all. And if I hadn't been there, might God have used someone else? Perhaps. But the point is, He didn't. He used me because He put me in the business and sent me there. The business was the reason I was on the plane and He gave me an opportunity to further His Kingdom purpose "along the way."

Another time, in Cincinnati, I returned from a lunch with several key engineers who were working on an important project with us. One of them, who was not directly a part of the group and had simply wandered by as we were leaving, joined us and called me aside.

"May I ask you a personal question?" he inquired.

"Sure," I replied.

"I noticed that you and your friend bowed your heads for a moment before you ate. Were you saying grace?"

"Yes, we were," I replied.

"Well, what religion are you?"

"I'm a Christian."

"I know," he said, "but what kind? Are you Catholic or Baptist or what?"

"I'm just a Christian," I said.

"What does that mean?"

"It means I believe in Jesus Christ as my Lord and Savior and I'm trying to learn to follow Him," I responded.

"I've never heard of anything like that. Would you be willing to come over to my house and tell my wife and me what it means?"

I didn't know at that point that he and his wife had seen an attorney that week and that they were discussing divorce. Nor did I know that he had been visiting the Jehovah's Witness church over the previous three weeks. I just bowed my head for about 10 seconds to give thanks before I ate. God took it all from there.

Paul and his wife both accepted Jesus into their hearts that night. They remain married to this day and, at last count (though it has been many years since we've talked), 24 more people have come to be a part of the family of God through them. I have no idea how many more have come by now, as the 24 are just those in their family!

I do know though, that if it hadn't been for business, I wouldn't have been in Cincinnati, Ohio at all. The business was the vehicle that took me there.

I once gave a Swedish man that I met in London (and later visited in Switzerland) a copy of . Lewis' *Mere Christianity* translated into Swedish. He read it and his faith was strengthened. He told me so when I later saw him in Illinois. All this as we negotiated a $500,000 fee and royalty agreement. I met him because of the business, of course.

> *What are your plans and dreams for ministry in your business?*

These are just a few examples that the Lord brought to mind. Only He knows how many others I may have missed, both in my recollection and along the way!

I could go on and on in sharing wonderful stories based on my years interacting with Christian marketplace leaders. There are tons of examples of all of the manifestations of Christian ministry that only happened because business was used to bring two lives together. These include: people claiming salvation, Christians being encouraged in the faith, and people who don't know God being given a demonstration of His unconditional love. Generally, these were a result of no special plan, just faithful followers of Christ doing business and relating to other people. That, as we all know, is all that business really is: people relating to and serving other people.

The process of doing business, by definition, brings us into contact with all kinds of people all of the time. We can't avoid it even though we might like to at times.

So, what are your plans and dreams for ministry in your business? How might you bring forth or apply the good news to your employees, customers, suppliers, and others you know or meet along the way? A hundred years from now this ministry impact will be the only part of the business that matters to us!

Our opportunities and calling are real and the possibilities are endless. Dream on my friend, and may your dreams lead you to produce much fruit.

1. Explain how you have seen your business, or any business, used to bring two lives together in such a way that the Gospel of Jesus Christ was delivered or applied.

_____

_____

_____

_____

_____

_____

_____

_____

2. What, in your opinion, are the key ingredients in using a business in this way?

_____

_____

_____

_____

_____

_____

_____

_____

3. In the same vein, what do you think are the greatest inhibitors?

_____

_____

_____

_____

_____

_____

_____

_____

CHAPTER 4

Basic Tools Used to Build Christian Testimony in Your Business

Let's revisit some basic foundational tools for building the work of God in and through our companies. These tools are not new nor the result of some special revelation. They are simple, available to all, and can be practiced in different ways by any believer in any company.

Jesus spoke of the need for proper foundations several times. One that comes to mind is found at the end of The Sermon on The Mount when He compared those men who build on strong or weak foundations. The man who built his house up on rock was seen as able to withstand the storms of life, while the man who built on sand could not and fell to the storm (Matthew 7:24-29). The implication is that the one was wise and endured, while the other was foolish and had only fleeting 'success'.

In the big picture of what we are all about in C12, success in the ministry dimension of our business is far more important than merely financial or material success. That is not to say that we are not interested in sustained financial growth and progress.

> Sow an act
> and you reap a habit;
> sow a habit
> and you reap a character;
> sow a character
> and you reap a destiny.
> G.C. Boardman

We are very diligent in working on this vital aspect of stewardship. In fact, long-term C12 members typically outperform their non-C12 industry peers as measured by sales and profit growth. But on a comparative basis, our success in these areas will be of great value to us only in terms of how we leverage it for eternal benefit since we will soon leave our companies and everything else in this world behind and go on home.

With this in mind, the following basic tools should be viewed as those designed to enhance the quality and scope of our success in building a strong Christian testimony in and through our businesses. There are at least eight such tools that have proven themselves over time.

The first tool is reverence for and submission to the written **Word of God** and its timeless principles. This seems pretty obvious, but many stumble here. Too many act as if they believe that the Bible and its teachings are okay for Sunday and perhaps Wednesday evenings, but have little or no relevance during business hours. Strong Christian testimony isn't likely to happen any better in a company ignoring God's Word than in a church with the same problem. The CEO or Owner is key here. Your reverence for the Bible, ability to conversationally apply its principles, and submission to its commands and truths in decision-making will lead the way in influencing the entire company's attitude. This sets the tone for how God's truth relates to others and their view of reality (i.e., what's desirable or acceptable) in the workplace.

Another key tool is the practice of **prayer** as an acknowledged and integral part of the business process. The use of our privilege to pray should be as normal in our business lives as it is in our practice at home and church. We should pray for our employees, customers, suppliers, and even our competitors. We should seek God's provision for future employees and customers. We should seek His will for decisions of all kinds, and we should not hide our prayer practice and reliance on God's grace and provision. We should acknowledge this openly when appropriate. Also, when He answers and we see His blessing, we should not be ashamed to publicly give thanks. If we practice one kind of prayer life at home and another type at work, then we are compromising and living a dualistic existence.

Our third tool involves a specific focus within a portion of our prayer life, expressing *a heart for the salvation of those who are lost*. We will not all be gifted evangelists or deeply involved in direct personal evangelism, but we must all share God's heart for saving the lost. We can see how much God cares about saving lost people if we look at the price He was willing to pay in order that it could happen. God didn't sacrifice His Son so that people could be healed or have demons cast out of them, or to impress us with miracles. Jesus did all that before He died on the cross. But before He died for us we were all lost and unable to save ourselves. Does God have a heart for evangelism? Of course He does, and we need to have one too. As His disciples and ambassadors, we are to "always be prepared to give an answer to everyone who asks you to give a reason for the hope that you have" (1 Peter 3:15 NIV). We each work out our part in the process of helping others know the Lord in various ways, but we must care about it and be alert to the opportunities that He may provide at work.

The fourth tool can help us remember these things during the heat of the everyday battle with the world, the flesh, and the devil that are always a part of the process. We need a written **Statement of Purpose** (also known as a Mission Statement) that actually works for us by possessing the following characteristics:

- clear, concise and easy to remember, so that we can easily use it as a day-to-day decision-making tool. If it is too long or complicated we won't use it and it becomes essentially worthless! A properly created Statement of Purpose is a working tool which should become well worn and tested by use.
- reflects the eternal purposes of our work in addition to the temporal. It should be written to remind us of our most important priorities first.
- your heart must be revealed honestly in your Statement of Purpose if it is to really work for you. It should inspire you and provide clear guidance as you engage in the process of running the company God has entrusted to you.

Tool number five is a **willingness to give from your increase**. Some may choose to give privately because of the structure of the corporation, but the 'attitude of gratitude' and willingness to share what is already God's is the point. Where possible, it is an advantage to give through the company. Obviously this isn't because a company can become holy or be saved or anything like that. Even though a company is an inanimate entity with no soul as such, it does have a culture and a prevailing 'spirit.' It's hard to define exactly what that aura or feeling within a company truly is, but let's call it a personality. A family unit is also an inanimate entity and families can only be saved one person at a time just like companies or churches. However, we've all experienced the sense of warmth we feel when we come into a loving and giving home or church. Our goal should be for others to feel that same sort of thing when they come into contact with our business. Having a giving (rather than a stingy) heart is a part of that. Companies definitely have personalities. The question is what kind of personality does your company exhibit?

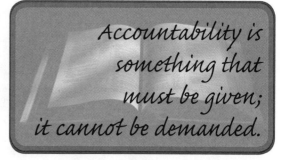

If it is really to work for you, your heart must be revealed honestly in your Statement of Purpose.

The **quality of our product or service** is a tool that will help build a strong platform for Christian testimony and ministry. People see us at least in part through their experience with our product. The Lord calls on us to do our work as unto Him (Colossians 3:23). For a Christian, this means to do the very best quality work that He enables us to do through the talents, abilities, and resources He gives us. In other words, we should be on a never-ending quest and commitment to excellence. Excellence for a Christian means being all He designed us to be without regard to how we may compare to anyone else. Others may have more talent or ability than we do and be able to outperform us seven days a week. That is not a problem for God. He only wants us to be all He created us to be and excellent compared only to our own potential and the opportunity He gives us to demonstrate it. The strength of our testimony in the marketplace, and the willingness in others to listen to us, will be highly influenced by how they perceive the quality of our product or service.

The last two tools are more personal as they have to do with our individual choices.

The seventh is the need to be in **accountable relationships**. In the Book of Proverbs there are over twenty references to the need for and value of Godly counsel. True Godly counsel can only come from those Godly persons who we are open and honest with us and to whom we are accountable. If we are not deeply transparent with our counselors, they are unable to deal with us from true knowledge

Accountability is something that must be given; it cannot be demanded.

of a situation or circumstance. We should mutually desire "speaking the truth in love" (Ephesians 4:15). If we are unwilling to thoughtfully and prayerfully consider and respond to their guidance, it will have no power in our lives.

So many well-meaning men and women have started wonderfully in the effort to create a life, ministry, or company to serve and honor God, only to later fall into sin or disgrace rooted in deception. Such sustained deception is typically made possible by their trying to "go it alone." To be a lone sheep means certain failure, as the wolves are too many and too strong. A wise man who has tried to help many of the famous Christian leaders who have fallen during the past generation claims that the single characteristic they share is that none of them were in truly accountable relationships with anyone during the years immediately prior to falling into the errors that ultimately snared them. Can we truly believe that we are spiritually stronger or better than they?

C12 offers an opportunity for the kind of accountable relationships we are talking about. We say opportunity because accountability is something that cannot be demanded, it must be given. C12 members must see the value and freedom in being open and honest with fellow members and decide to make themselves mutually accountable. The quality, integrity and depth of those things that they choose to share and be held accountable for will greatly influence and shape the quality, integrity, depth and testimony of their lives!

The final tool is a commitment on your part to **personal spiritual growth and development**. Your company will never rise above the level of spiritual maturity or commitment of your leadership. As Owner or CEO, you are the leader in the eyes of your people and before God. If your spiritual growth is not a major concern to you, it is far less likely to be a priority for any of your people, at least while they're at work. You and I are the spiritual leaders of our companies; it is not something that can be delegated. If we don't lead here it won't happen.

The methods of personal spiritual development are well known. They're not mysterious or ethereal. You and I have been exhorted towards them as long as we have been Christians. They include: prayer for our daily needs, consistent intercession for others, thanksgiving, confession and repentance of known sin, seeking God's will for our lives and circumstances, Bible study and meditation, spending time in worship and fellowship with like-minded believers, and working to spread the Gospel of our Lord Jesus Christ. You know the ways as well as I do. These have been the Lord's means of grace or spiritual disciplines for the past two millennia. There are no shortcuts.

At the risk of being labelled dogmatic, I believe that the single most powerful tool

> *Spending time with Him is more important than spending time doing ANYTHING ELSE!*

available to us is the habit of engaging in daily quiet time with God. Every single area of our lives depends on and flows out of our relationship with Him. Spending time with Him, and developing an increasing intimacy with our Lord, is more important than spending time doing ANYTHING ELSE. The biography of every great Christian reveals the truth of this assertion. And, as painful as it may be to our comfort, the testimony of our forefathers in the faith is that it was the first thing that they did EVERY DAY! Can we really expect similar results to those they experienced from dissimilar actions?

No, the sober truth is that each of our spiritual conditions exactly corresponds to the price we are willing to pay in terms of diligence in our daily pursuit of Him and His ways. We get from God exactly what we decide that we want in terms of our relationship with Him. He has already made every provision we need to grow as much as we will. He is always ready to be with us as our Father, instructor, counselor, guide, brother, confessor, comforter, lover and friend. Any shortfall we experience is never due to His part or provision. If we truly want to grow, we can! He will always do His part! Always!

The hardest and perhaps most sobering question that we can ask ourselves is, "Do I really want to be ALL that God wants me to be?" The answer to that question is being demonstrated by our lives and choices each and every day. And, our companies show it. They are now, and will always be, a reflection of our true heart. It may not be easy to hear, that but it's true. Of course, our hearts can change once we realize a need to change, repent and begin the next step of our faith walk. How much change, you ask? As much as our faith and obedience will allow!

So there we are, eight tools we can use to build a destiny as Christian business leaders. You may have noticed by now that these eight are the same, with only a little different phrasing or wordsmithing, which we might use to discuss spiritual progress of any kind. At least it is sincerely hoped that you will find this to be true. God really doesn't have radically different sets of plans for different areas of our lives. He has only one plan, purpose and set of eternal principles which are to be worked out in necessarily different ways in different places.

These tools are those He has given to us for profitable use. While we must decide to use them or not, He has made them available to all. Can we succeed by using only some of them? Perhaps we can. But if we do, it will be a lot harder and less fruitful than if we use them all. It's like building a house. You might build a house using only a hammer. It might even ultimately end up being a beautiful house but it is very doubtful that a house built with only a hammer could be constructed as easily or as well as one built with all the tools designed for the purpose (e.g., saws, planes, T-squares, nails, screws, screwdrivers, etc.). While such an example might seem somewhat ridiculous, it is no more ridiculous than trying to build your Christian testimony in the company that God has given you without all the tools He has sovereignly provided for the purpose!

Worksheet

1. In my company, how do I demonstrate respect for and submission to God's Word?

   _____
   _____
   _____
   _____
   _____
   _____

2. How does prayer play a role in my company? Are my prayer practices the same at work as at home or church?

   _____
   _____
   _____
   _____
   _____
   _____

3. In my company, how do I share my concern for the lost being saved?

   _____
   _____
   _____
   _____
   _____
   _____

4. Is our Statement of Purpose a true daily help in making clear decisions and building Christian testimony in and through the company?

   _____
   _____
   _____
   _____
   _____
   _____

5. Is the financial giving done through my company truly representative of my heart?

    _____
    _____
    _____
    _____
    _____
    _____

6. How do customers see a testimony to my Christian faith in the quality of the work that we do for them?

    _____
    _____
    _____
    _____
    _____
    _____

7. Am I truly accountable to anyone for things that are really important to me and my spiritual, social, professional, and family life ?

    _____
    _____
    _____
    _____
    _____
    _____

8. Am I doing all I now know to do to grow in intimacy with my Lord?

    _____
    _____
    _____
    _____
    _____
    _____

Strategy for Ministry

In his highly influential 1989 best-seller, *The Seven Habits of Highly Effective People*, Stephen Covey exhorts us in Habit One to "BE PROACTIVE." In discussing his seven "paradigms" prescription for "restoring the character ethic" in our personal, organizational, and community interactions, he bases all the Habits on this first one.

Covey contrasts proactivity with reactivity. A proactive person recognizes that there are basically only two kinds of things that concern us in life, those we can do something about, and those we can do nothing about. He realizes that he has the primary responsibility power to choose his direction and focus his efforts. The proactive person also recognizes that to focus on things that he has no control over is wasteful and foolish. And so he chooses to use his ability to act on the things he can influence and resists the temptation to worry or spin his wheels too much about things he can't control.

A proactive person is able to see things in relative priority, recognizing that some things are more important than others and therefore worthy of more attention. With this in mind, the proactive person initiates positive actions and makes choices to promote the purposes and values he or she holds to be most important.

Reactive people, on the other hand, are primarily controlled by and preoccupied with their circumstances. They are like a reed blown by the wind. Whichever way the wind blows, they move for that moment, distracted perhaps until the wind changes again. Reactive people are like thermometers, reacting to whatever environment they encounter. They essentially reflect their surrounding conditions and are temporarily changed.

Proactive people, in contrast, are much more like thermostats. Thermostats control the environment as much as they can. No matter what the environment is doing, the thermostat is doing all it can to influence it to a predetermined or desired condition. A proactive person chooses what he or she will react to and what they won't. Their reactions are based on predetermined priorities and values. Proactive people make a plan and work their plan.

Reactive people plan to plan and hope to plan. But if they ever actually make a plan, the first fire shoves it to the back burner where it is soon forgotten. We see this reality worked out all around us in the business world. We all know people who simply show up each day and spend the whole day putting out fires. Their 'plan' is to react to the first phone call or demands from staff or customers and to continue through the day reacting to events as they occur. They don't think of it as reactivity, but that is exactly what it is. They run breathlessly from one situation to the next, constantly reacting to what jumps up in front of them, never stopping long enough to consider priorities or long-term value. They finish the day and fall into bed exhausted from a fight they never can win, only to get up and start all over again the next day. Classically, this is termed a reactive management style. It never works well for long. Perhaps you know someone who uses it!

Let's switch gears for a moment and think about the concept that our businesses are a gift from God. He gives them to us to be used for His glory and as a platform for His ministry. This is His call and plan for our lives. With a Biblical concept of reality, we agree that we are stewards and managers of God's property. With all we have or control, we serve at His pleasure.

Think about the parables that Jesus taught about the talents (Matthew 25) and the minas (Luke 19). The main message in each involves the requirement to be faithful and profitable in the use of all that we have been given. In each parable, the servants were only criticized when they did not use what they had been given to gain a profit. The simplest and (in this writer's opinion) least important application of this teaching pertains to money.

Yes, God does expect us to be good stewards of money. But there are things of much greater value and infinitely greater importance than money. Jesus said money was a little thing and directed us to be faithful in the use of things more important than money. He described these other things as "true riches."

These parables each refer to our common opportunity to participate with God in building His Kingdom. We build His Kingdom by sharing His truth and love in the circumstances in which He places us. That's what Jesus did and that's what we are to do as His followers. He gives us talents and minas in the form of businesses and families and local churches. He says to us, "Do business until I come." What He means is, "Promote my interests as long as I ask you to."

He has established a system of eternal rewards that will be given to those who faithfully earn them. That's right, earn them! While we may be already saved, eternal rewards result from appropriate action based upon obedience.

Our rewards will be based on what we have done in obedience, with the provision and potential He has given us, toward faithfully helping God to build His Kingdom.

The largest single portion of our waking hours is spent 'at work' running the company that God has entrusted to us. We spend more time there – for most of us, roughly half of our waking hours – than anywhere else. Therefore, our potential to impact people and participate in building the Kingdom is, for us, greater in the marketplace than anywhere else. We are there more, we have more discretionary control over both what is done and how it is done, and we have been placed there by God for the very purpose. We clearly have a high potential opportunity for a significant 'ministry of presence'!

The relevant question isn't whether such ministry opportunity exists. Rather it is whether we will seize it and prosper in it! This brings us back to where we started. You wouldn't be a part of C12 if you didn't have at least a general assent or agreement with the understandings expressed above. Our hearts are knit together in the desire to faithfully and effectively do those things God has chosen us to do. Since, at least for now, that includes leading a company, we have a specific sacred role to play in the unfolding of His sovereign plan. One hundred or a thousand years from now these issues will *still* be important to us! Participating with God in obedience to His will, through a unified life of stewardship and worship, will always be THE MOST IMPORTANT THING.

So, at work, how are *you* doing? Do you have a clue? Do you have anywhere near as good an idea of how well you are doing with God's work as you do about driving your sales, profitability or debt-to-equity ratio? Do you spend as much time planning for ministry as for revenue growth or advertising? Do you spend as much time evaluating the results of your ministry efforts as you do looking at orders, collections or cash flow? Since we've already established that in a hundred or a million years from now God's work will be all that is important, why not?

Most of us have no difficulty accepting the value of proactivity as it applies to our immediate circumstances. It's easy for most of us to see the waste and ineffectiveness due to reactionary management practices in our business lives. But most of us are content to rely almost entirely upon simple reaction to conduct any ministry in and through our companies. If an obvious opportunity jumps up and hits us in the nose, we'll usually do something about it, unless, of course, we're distracted by something more important like a sales call or a supplier delivery problem.

There *are* many things we can't control about our ministry, whether at work, at home, or in the most remote jungle village. We certainly don't know how it will be received in advance of doing it. We can't control how others will perceive our message or efforts as they are done or even later upon reflection. We can't always see the fruit of our efforts and we may not currently even understand why God wants it done at all.

But we, and only we, can control whether we do it, in faith, or not. The farmer can't control the weather, make the crops grow faster, or reap the harvest before its time. But he, and only he, can sow the seed and plow the ground. Some things God will take care of, but some things the farmer must do. He must plan and put in the effort to plant. He must cultivate and fertilize. If he does his part, God will give the growth. If the farmer doesn't act with diligence, God can't (or maybe more accurately, won't). The Lord is certainly able to provide in a myriad of ways, but He clearly desires to work through us!

Who will do the ministry in your company? If you don't lead it or at least encourage it, it's likely that no one will. If you don't take proactive responsibility for it, who will? Can you afford to be purely reactive in this vital area? Do you really think it wise to 'just let what happens happen' and count it all up later? Most Christians are doing just that, day by day. They blithely lead their lives and businesses, making no plan and having no strategy.

It really makes no sense to leave the most important things in the hands of chance and spend great effort on the things that will only eventually burn up anyway. It makes no sense, but that's what we typically do. Be encouraged by the words of the late missionary, Jim Elliot, who said, "He is no fool who gives what he cannot keep to gain that which he cannot lose."

One of C12's maxims is that "what we spend time on tends to improve." If the

> *It makes no sense to leave the most important things in the hands of chance and spend the greater effort on the things that will eventually burn.*

ministry in and through your company isn't what you would like it to be, the chances are really good that you aren't spending enough time or the right kind of focus on it. As with all sound long-term business endeavors, we need to effectively plan and then work to execute the plan. In fact, a strategic plan for the work of God in and through your company is more important, with greater value to you, than any other business plan you can conceive or create.

A good proactive plan involves: (1) **vision** (Stephen Covey calls it "beginning with the end in mind") regarding where you want to go, (2) **strategy** or a road map of how you are going to get there and (3) **tactics** regarding what you will do today to support your vision with specific deliverables and accountabilities that can be measured. The effort you put into making and executing such a ministry plan will pay you back forever!

C12 encourages you to produce an **Action Plan** for ministry in your business. Such an Action Plan is based on the same principles we use to do a "Business Plan":

- Understand the vision and purpose of the enterprise.
- Identify and calibrate the potential of our served market niche(s).
- Brainstorm/strategize our plans and tactics.
- Set our goals and objectives.
- Establish accountability, reporting procedures and begin to execute!

To prepare for the next step, work through the questions on the worksheet that follows.

1. Does your Statement of Purpose reflect eternal values, qualities, and objectives?

    _____

2. What is your plan for accomplishing God's purpose in giving you a company to run for Him?

    _____
    _____
    _____
    _____

3. What are your spiritual gifts?

    _____

4. How are you using them through your company?

    _____
    _____
    _____

5. Who else in your company has God given you to work with to accomplish His purpose in and through the business? How might you enlist their efforts and encourage or excite their sense of ministry purpose?

    _____
    _____
    _____

6. How much time have you spent in the last year planning to do things in your company that might have eternal value? What are you working on in your business today that you think might be important to you in 20, 50, 100, or 1000 years?

    _____
    _____
    _____

7. Are you really willing to leave it for later or in the hands of chance?

    ◯ Yes   ◯ No

Assessing Your Current Status & Developing Your Action Plan

Today we will outline a five-step process to develop a sound Action Plan for effective ministry and then give ourselves a check-up to assess our current standing on each of the five components. This is not a prescriptive 'one-size-fits-all' exercise. Each of us have been uniquely gifted to lead businesses with differing opportunities and constraints. Our hope is that you will be challenged to seek those opportunities the Lord has sovereignly called you to address.

Let's begin our Action Plan by reviewing (or creating) your **Mission** or **Purpose Statement**. For our purposes here we will use these terms interchangeably. The real acid test of a great Purpose Statement is that it both includes and excites your sense of ministry. The foundation for having effective ministry in and through our businesses is a Mission Statement that is effective in promoting ministry! This simple truth is undergirded by several key ingredients. A good Mission Statement must be:

1. **Inspiring.** It needs to excite us in our heart of hearts. Ideally, a good Mission Statement will function in our lives much as the cry *"Semper Fi!"* functions for a Marine. It says in a few words what grips us and moves us to action.

2. **Short and easy to remember.** If it is too long it will be unworkable, unmemorable, and fall into disuse. It needs to be concise, ideally just one sentence or two at the most.

3. Constructed so that it may be used as a **decision-making tool**, or arbiter, so that the daily decisions needed to operate the business accordingly can be informed, evaluated or measured by it. A Mission Statement that is not used routinely in the decision-making processes of a business is of little consequence. A really good Mission Statement permeates an organization, serving as a 'plumb line' used to guide actions and decisions even to the lowest levels of the organization.

4. **Reflect your heart** as the owner or chief executive. If you don't own it and model it, no one else will own it either!

5. Continually inspire, reinforce, and **excite your sense of ministry.** Having a Mission Statement that talks about universal operating characteristics such as quality, excellence, relationships and service is great, but indistinguishable from purely secular businesses. Somehow, a truly effective Mission Statement needs to stir our hearts for the main purpose of God, through us, in business. Although this can be done in many ways so as to increase our effectiveness in ministry, it must remind us that ministry is an essential and integrated element of our business.

The following are some examples of Mission Statements created by others. You may gain some insights and ideas for your own adoption by reviewing them.

- "To change the world by bringing forth the Kingdom of God in the marketplace through the companies and lives of those He calls to run businesses for Him." *The C12 Group, LLC*

- "To honor God in all we do, to help people develop, to pursue excellence, to grow profitably." *The ServiceMaster Company*

- "Serving Him by Serving You" *POS Company*

- "This business exists to bring honor and glory to God and to do business in such a way that His Son, Jesus Christ, will be able to say, 'Well done faithful servants'." *S.H. Mack & Company*

- "ROC Carbon is the premiere service-oriented Carbon manufacturer, worldwide, providing quality products and exceptional service that draws attention to the reason we exist —to know God and to make Him known." *ROC Carbon*

- "Our purpose is to glorify God through our commitment to integrity, excellence, service to others, and a high regard for every person with whom we have business." *Cooper Electrical Construction Company*

- "The purpose of King's Wholesale Florists is to glorify God by the way we serve our customers, care for our employees, treat our suppliers, and help our community." *King's Wholesale Florists Co., Inc.*

- "Moving in the Spirit of Jesus Christ by (1) Investing in Relationships, (2) Striving for Quality Service, (3) Commitment to Integrity, and (4) Promoting Eternal Values." *Spirit Movers, Inc.*

- "Precerche Life Sciences exists to honor Christ and glorify His name by utilizing the skills, talents, resources and capabilities that He has entrusted to us to benefit the physical health and well-being of humanity while fulfilling the mandate of the Great Commission through business." *Precerche Life Sciences, LP*

- "Sharing the love of Christ while providing unique services to the manufactured housing industry." *Newby Management Corporation*

- "Committed to honor the Greatest Designer, God, and to make him known by building relationships and producing quality design." *Maddox & Associates, P.A.*

- "The purpose of our business is to glorify God by serving you the most excellent products possible, that by this our Lord Jesus might be able to say, 'Well done, my good and faithful servant'." *Dallas 1 Construction & Development*

- "Sharing the love of Christ while building homes and relationships with excellence." *Pruett Builders*

Reread the five qualities of an effective Purpose or Mission Statement in the previous section. Rate your existing Mission Statement on a scale of 1-10, with 10 being high, against the qualities given.

1   2   3   4   5   6   7   8   9   10

Note: If you don't have one, or are dissatisfied with your current Statement of Purpose, please use the worksheet provided in Appendix A.

The second component of an integrated plan for effective ministry is to **Know the Target Markets**. This equates to much of the marketing process in our business.

To be effective in business we have to have a real knowledge of *who* our customers are and *where* they are before we can even begin to find out their needs and wants and to develop strategies to supply them. Knowing the size and location of our target markets is basic to understanding our company's potential and essential to our long-term success.

Looking at our company's potential in the ministry dimension requires the same perspective. If we consider our product for ministry in our business to be the Gospel of our Lord Jesus Christ in all its applications and manifestations, and our business to be a vehicle or conduit for the distribution of this product, we first need to know what the attributes of our market are in terms of location and size. Establishing tastes and preferences comes only after we know the fundamentals of scope and location.

Each business has a highly specific natural market for its ministry which is uniquely accessible to the business. This market requires no additional effort to establish. It is made up of all those who we already interact with and do business with in any way. We call this our "circle of influence." Every business has this unique group of possible customers for the Gospel of our Lord Jesus Christ. No two are the same. These are the people we come into contact with during the normal course of business. They buy from us, sell to us, deliver us goods and services, compete with us and work with us. They are all around us every day. We don't have to exert extra effort or expense to go look for them as we are already in relationship, or trying to be, with them. The Gospel is shared through relational contact, just as business is. People do business with people. People share the Gospel with people. Our goal is to learn to do both in one seamless process. But first we need to know our market, which is all those we 'touch' in a given year.

Identifying My Mission Field

Do you know your market? Let's see. Fill in the worksheet answering each question on an annual basis.

Number

1. How many employees do you have? _____
   a. Multiply your employees by two, as they have families. _____
   b. How many others ask you for a job in a year? _____

2. How many customers do you serve annually? _____
   a. How many others do you call on who don't buy? _____
   b. How many other people see your ads, billboards, company sign or literature each year? _____

3. How many suppliers of all kinds do you use in your business in a year? _____
   a. How many others call on you that you don't currently use? _____

4. How many competitors know your company? _____

5. How many other people do you know just because of business? _____

My Total Markeplace Ministry Mission Field _____

*Number of Individual **Target Market Segments*** _____

This number of 'touches' and these target market segments represent your unique mission field or market for ministry of the Gospel. You will relate to them in various ways during the next year and perhaps every year for the foreseeable future. How you may or may not choose to share the Gospel with them is not the point here. The point is that they are there and that you can if you choose. Average church membership in America is less than 100. How does your mission field compare? The average church will see less than 75 new people each year. How many will you contact?

Do **you** know your target market? If this is old news to you, give yourself a 10. If it's old news but you aren't doing anything with it, take 5 off. If you've never thought of this before and are motivated to take action, take a 5 for thinking about it now.

| 1 | 2 | 3 | 4 | 5 | 6 | 7 | 8 | 9 | 10 |

Note: A copy of this worksheet is provided in Appendix B for use with your team.

After we know who comprises our target market, our next step is to develop our strategy for presenting our 'product' to them and helping them buy it. It is equivalent to making a sales plan. We call this third component **Brainstorming Methods and Options**. This is where our creative abilities are really engaged. The challenge is to learn to do things in the course of doing business that will allow those who God is drawing, or has drawn, to Himself, or who need His love and mercy, to identify themselves to us, and avail themselves of our product. To do so **we** most often have to take the first step by identifying ourselves as having the product and being willing to share it. This is Jesus' 'Good Shepherd' model for outreach (John 10) as contrasted with the failed 'Little Bo Peep' model (i.e., "leave them alone and they'll come home...")!

The question becomes, "How do we do that as we do business, relating to our market in a business way, with as great a degree of excellence and professionalism possible, and at the same time having as a concurrent purpose sharing the Gospel?"

One well-known example of sharing the Gospel integrated with the routine conduct of the business is Buck Knives, who for decades have included a small printed Gospel testimony in the box with their product. From the multiple vertical file cabinets full of letters and testimonies of those touched by these Christ-centered messages, we might ask the following: between the knife and the Gospel message, which is the true product (and purpose) of Buck Knives? Arguably, the knife is the vehicle which delivers the real product, one of eternal value!

To reach out to those we touch will challenge all of our the creative abilities. One of the most valuable and successful ways of engaging these abilities is through the use of creative brainstorming. We can begin to utilize this potential by drawing on the others God has given us to work with, inviting them to join us in imagining what might be done to share the work of ministry as a part of our ongoing work relationship.

We may do this with several groups or only one. For instance, we might initially choose to work with a group of key Christian managers. Or we may choose to include the entire team in the process. That decision varies with each company. The point of this component is to do it and engage others in creatively seeking options and methods for applying the ministry of the Gospel as we do business. The definition of ministry in simplified form is three-fold; (1) **salvation** – introducing others to God who don't know Him, (2) **sanctification** – helping those who already know Him to get to know Him better, and (3) **service** – sharing God's love and mercy with those who are in need. We can use many different techniques based on our own preferences to do the actual brainstorming (e.g., force field analysis, modified Delphi analysis, red light-green light, storyboarding, affinity diagrams using sticky notes, etc.) to develop possibilities, but the point is to do it. In a typical company such brainstorming might easily generate a list of 15 to 30 possibilities. This third step is simply to create a list of options, possibilities, or methods for any or all of the three categories of ministry. Participants should be encouraged to be creative and let their ideas flow freely. Their suggestions will not be judged at this point, merely sought after and collected.

Have you done this? Have you done it lately? Rate yourself. If you have never asked anyone what they thought about anything give yourself a 1. If you did this once a while ago, but never did anything with the results, take a 0. If you did it once to get started and put some things in play, but haven't revisited the results or the process for a couple of years take a 5. If you do creative brainstorming for the purpose of improving the ministry in and through your business at least once each year, take an 8. If you do it each year with your team and follow through on it, you are a 10! Now rate yourself.

1   2   3   4   5   6   7   8   9   10

Note: Use Appendices C and D to assist here.

Component four is to **Establish Definite Goals and Consistent Actions**. Here we take the 1, 2, or 3 best ideas (i.e., most exciting, easiest to implement, most easily doable actions) from the list created in our brainstorming session and make a written plan to do them. In this selection process, look for things to do that are appealing to you and consistent with your spiritual gifts and interests as well as those of your team. In order for this plan to be effective its supporting goals and execution should reflect several important qualities, as follows:

1. The plan must be **specific** in terms of what the actions will be, when they will start, who will be responsible, and at what points in time results will be evaluated.

2. It must have **measurable** results as its objective.

3. It must be **action-oriented** and **realistic**.

4. You should establish a defined **time frame**.

5. It must be **integrated** into the strategic plan of the company and treated as equal to every other part of the business plan. By this we mean that if you check sales, profit or market share for your business each month, the results of your ministry activities listed here should be checked as frequently and seriously.

6. There must be **accountability** assigned and applied. Just as a business plan is worthless if there is no accountability for executing it, so will a ministry plan be. We can expect what we are willing to inspect and what we pay attention to always gets better. Ultimately God will hold each of us accountable for how we use the opportunity He provides, so we might as well accept this fact and make ourselves accountable now.

If the individual ministry initiative is something that you have never done before you will have to make some assumptions and "best guess" scenarios to get started. Just take the idea and ask yourself, "What result would I hope to achieve in one year?" As a simple example, you might decide to put a One-Year Bible in your reception area, opened to each day's date. And you might think that if one person asked about it each quarter you would be thrilled. Your goal becomes to place the Bible, train your receptionist to turn the pages daily and direct inquiries to you, track inquiries, and record and report them monthly.

A tracking form, chart, or spreadsheet can be used to identify actions and record results. Discussion of your progress should be integrated with other important business performance reporting as you review metrics for various functional responsibilities within the business.

So, how definite are your ministry goals? How consistent are your actions? Rate yourself. If you have a written plan, a project spreadsheet to track the results of ministry activities, review your results as often as you look at your firm's profit and loss results, and if you have been doing so for at least a full year, you are a 10! If you did this once, a few years ago, have looked at the results occasionally, don't have a form, and are convicted about it now, take a 6. If you've seen this idea before, but never done anything about it, you are a 2. If you've never seen anything like this before but are excited about it, you are a 4. If you've never done it but are excited and ready to set some goals take a 5. If you never intend to do anything like this, well, why are you here? Rate yourself in terms of the specificity of your goals and the consistency of your actions and follow-through.

| 1 | 2 | 3 | 4 | 5 | 6 | 7 | 8 | 9 | 10 |

Note: Use Appendix E to help you better define specific action steps.

The fifth component is to **Measure and Monitor Results and Make Adjustments**. This is the actualization of the first four components and is actually begun during in the goal-setting portion of component four. Once the goals for actions to be taken are established and methods for measuring progress towards the goals are agreed upon, there must be accountability established. This enables ongoing evaluation and helpful adjustments to be made based on current results. For instance, in the example we used, if your action step is to place a One-Year Bible in the reception area, you would train your receptionist to respond to anyone asking why you have the Bible on display to say, "The owner of this business has instructed me to tell anyone who asks, that he considers the Bible to be the most important book he has ever read, and to ask them if they would like to speak to him and find out why he feels that way. Would you like an appointment to speak to him?" The receptionist would then record the inquiry and the response on a form that would be reviewed each month along with all other periodic reports or perhaps collected on a consolidated "Ministry Report Form" along with other ministry efforts. This step relates to points 5 and 6 above. A high-performing person or team needs to be actively engaged in measuring and monitoring results and, if needed, making adjustments on an ongoing basis.

Finally, rate your ministry plan implementation. Is anyone watching? Do you have specific goals for whatever actions you are taking? Is anyone responsible for recording the results and reporting them to you? Rate yourself.

| 1 | 2 | 3 | 4 | 5 | 6 | 7 | 8 | 9 | 10 |

Worksheet

Total your ratings on the five components of developing an integrated Action Plan for effective ministry and divide by five to get your average rating.

Component	Rating
1. **Mission or Purpose Statement**	_____
2. **Know the Target Markets**	_____
3. **Brainstorming Methods and Options**	_____
4. **Establish Definite Goals and Consistent Actions**	_____
5. **Measure and Monitor Results and Make Adjustments**	_____

Average _____

This is a unique C12 exercise. There isn't a lot of data to use in commenting on what constitutes a strong or weak rating. We do know that these five components, if consistently applied, will have a powerful effect on the quality and consistency of ministry done in and through any business. So, we'll leave it with you. Honestly, what do you think? What should be the acceptable standard or minimum average rating? Of course it makes a difference just where we are in our exposure to the concept. Scripturally, we understand that those who know more will be held to a higher standard than those who know less. So maybe there is no single right answer other than that which is between each of us and God. In fact, let's leave it there, between you and God! Decide what your rating should be and compare that number to what it is at the moment. Work out any difference and revised expectations with Him.

Within the ranks of long-term C12 member companies, we have the privilege of being encouraged by several firms which have a greater evangelical impact, as measured by adult conversions, than that of all but the healthiest mega-churches. More than one C12 firm of roughly 100 employees report salvations averaging 25 per year as they faithfully minister through their growing enterprises. No doubt about it, diligence in this vital area is rewarded with much fruit!

Like any plan, your ministry plan needs to have a starting point and regular ongoing evaluation of key metrics. So, when will **you** start? If you've already begun, consider 'going deeper' in your active leadership by referring to Appendix F: A Formula for Ministry HyperGrowth. May your life and leadership glorify our Lord!

Appendices

Statement of Purpose

My Mission is to _____

_____

by _____

_____

The Purpose of my business is to _____

_____

_____

by _____

_____

Say it in your own words _____

_____

_____

_____

Try again _____

_____

_____

_____

Once more _____

_____

_____

_____

Final time _____

_____

_____

_____

Identifying My Mission Field

Do you know your market? Let's see. Fill in the worksheet answering each question on an annual basis.

1. How many employees do you have?   _____
   a. Multiply your employees by two, as they have families.   _____
   b. How many others ask you for a job in a year?   _____

2. How many customers do you serve annually?   _____
   a. How many others do you call on who don't buy?   _____
   b. How many other people see your ads, billboards, company sign or literature each year?   _____

3. How many suppliers of all kinds do you use in your business in a year?   _____
   a. How many others call on you that you don't currently use?   _____

4. How many competitors know your company?   _____

5. How many other people do you know just because of business?   _____

My Total Markeplace Ministry Mission Field   _____

Number of Individual **Target Market Segments**   _____

Brainstorming the Possibilities

Looking at the 'target markets' of your Marketplace Ministry Mission Field, ask the question, "If money were no object and we wanted to reach out with Christian ministry through our business contacts and relationships, what things could we do?" Use a brainstorming process to create a raw list of as many ideas as you can that might be done to promote or demonstrate Christian Ministry through your business. You can do this alone, with a close council of advisors, the entire employee team, your management team, or like-minded staff members. List the ideas below. Be sure not to judge the ideas as they flow, just collect them for now. We will evaluate them later.

1. _____
2. _____
3. _____
4. _____
5. _____
6. _____
7. _____
8. _____
9. _____
10. _____
11. _____
12. _____
13. _____
14. _____
15. _____
16. _____
17. _____
18. _____
19. _____
20. _____

101 Ministry Options

1. Prominently display your C12 member plaque with its Scriptural encouragement.

2. Establish written Biblical principles and values as a priority for your firm.

3. Prepare a mission statement that identifies you as a Christian business with a ministry objective. Put it on your business card and literature.

4. Provide Christian worldview seminars for employees, suppliers and the community.

5. Provide a Christian life/business resource library for your employees (e.g., tapes and videos on current topics, business issues and family matters).

6. Invite other business CEOs/Owners into C12.

7. Provide a chaplain for your employees (contact Corporate Chaplains of America).

8. Send children of employees to Christian camps.

9. Use Christian motivational speakers at company meetings.

10. Open and/or close company meetings with prayer and thanksgiving.

11. Have annual supplier and customer appreciation outings with a Kingdom message (e.g., testimonies, company purpose, gospel presentation, etc.).

12. Send employees and spouses to Family Life Seminar.

13. Use special seasons (e.g., Christmas, Easter, Thanksgiving, New Year) to send cards or letters with tactful Gospel messages to employees, suppliers, and customers.

14. Give away One-Year Bibles or other helpful study/application Bibles.

15. Share your views on current events or personal challenges in a monthly newsletter or employee letter. Make it Biblical but not preachy.

16. Promote joining a learning/accountability group of peers.

17. Give children's devotionals or Christian storybooks to employees for their children and grandchildren.

18. Use some of your firm's profits to support local ministries, especially those that help the poor.

19. Send your key people to seminars and conferences where they can relate to other business and professional leaders.

20. Lead a small group study or mentor individual employees on Christian values.

21. Teach employees financial planning, including giving from a Biblical perspective.

22. Have profit sharing of some kind and help them learn to plan for the future.

23. Provide educational recognition and scholarships for the children of employees.

24. Host a supplier appreciation banquet. Show them you value them as persons. Pay them on time.

25. Model application of Scripture in business. Look for "teachable moments" to use for illustrations.

26. Have a "Christ-centered" Christmas party.

27. Recognize Biblical fruitfulness in employees.

28. Release employees to do ministry on company time.

29. Sponsor a Christian radio program.

30. Pray daily for employees, customers, suppliers, and competitors.

31. Have Christian magazines and a Bible in your waiting area.

32. Display Christian paintings, pictures, Scripture, etc.

33. Play Christian music during your telephone system's "on hold" time.

34. Include tasteful evangelical tracts with invoices, payments, etc.

35. Have a company picnic with shared testimonies.

36. Set up a prayer box for employees and patrons to submit requests.

37. Pray for your immediate marketplace and surrounding businesses.

38. Have a compassion resource or help-line directory in your office to guide those you come in contact with who may need directions in getting assistance.

39. Establish a weekly prayer time and/or Bible study during lunch or off-hours.

40. Have a service to dedicate your business, new building, acquisition or team to God.

41. Hold "open houses" to share what drives your business with others.

42. Hire disadvantaged people who have gone through a life-skills course and need employment.

43. Commit to giving liberally from the business to help promote the Gospel locally.

44. Provide discounted/free services to local pastors and other Christian leaders.

45. Lend your employees to a local ministry that needs administrative help.

46. Conduct a drive for baby items for local pregnancy care centers. Throw a baby shower for one or more of the women committed to keeping her baby.

47. Include a small gift item when you bill your customers to show God's love. Items

such as Testamints and other creative candies can be found in most Christian bookstores.

48. Sponsor employees to attend a Christian concert or seminar with a block of tickets.

49. Host a luncheon on Boss' Day or Administrative Professionals' Day in your marketplace and share your testimony.

50. Share the resumes of good Christian employment prospects you may not be able to hire with other companies. The idea is to have these Christian employees understand that God is placing them to be a witness.

51. Bless your competitor through positive/high standards and 'reaching out'.

52. Assist struggling businesses in your vicinity as a mentor or with specific help.

53. When giving out paychecks, write a personal note of appreciation to the employee.

54. Provide financial management seminars using God's Word for your employees and others so they can stay out of debt and use their money wisely.

55. Make a list of names of family members of your employees with their ages, birthdays, anniversaries, or special interest, and send a Scriptural note on special days. Encourage fellow employees to remember each other.

56. Conduct a "Carefest" week. Each day is a different day of caring in a specific way.

57. Provide business card sized "handouts" for employees to use to bless others.

58. Locate a Christian marriage seminar and pay for employees to attend.

59. Get with other businesses and put on an appreciation banquet for the various compassion ministries in your community.

60. When a customer has paid his bill in full, send and invoice with a little note that says, "Good news! You are PAID IN FULL. These were the same words Jesus spoke when He hung on the cross for your sins."

61. Retail businesses can put up a sign that reads: "Ask about our exchange policy." When customers ask, let them know about the actual policy you may have, and then ask if they would like to hear about the best exchange policy on the planet—how Christ provides the greatest exchange, His righteousness and eternal life for our sin and faith.

62. List Jesus Christ as owner of your business and you as steward on your letterhead.

63. Take employees out to breakfast or lunch just to get to know them better personally.

64. Develop a prayer "hit list" by having your Bible study group compile a top-10 list of people to pray for.

65. Donate computers or equipment to local after-school programs to teach skills and God's love.

66. Pay your employees for time involved with a community outreach such as Habitat for Humanity or a similar activity.

67. Maintain an emergency "deacon's fund", fueled by all employees and a small portion of net profits, to address occasional emergency needs of those in need/company stakeholders and rotate administration among teams of 'like-minded' employees.

68. Help seniors to become computer literate. In exchange, ask them to mentor youth or volunteer for small ministries that need help.

69. Prepare several Christ-centered ways to answer the question, "What do you do for a living?"

70. Host a lunch for local area pastors.

71. Write out a salvation/business testimony that simply tells others how God has blessed your life.

72. Provide a baby-sitter so a single mom who works for you can go out. Buy a movie ticket and dinner for her and a friend or offer to take her out with your spouse.

73. Give away free stuff (bottled water, cold soda) along with a care card that explains why you are doing it.

74. List your "credentials" as AfC (Ambassador for Christ) after your name on correspondence and business cards.

75. "Adopt" local community folks in need (i.e., widows, orphans, families of orphans, refugees, foster children) and provide on-going prayer, encouragement, and practical/relational support.

76. Provide pre-retirement counseling and planning seminars. Also consider keeping "alumni" involved with continuing community ministry activities.

77. Enable local Kingdom ministries to use helpful company resources and infrastructure "at cost."

78. Occasionally "test" employees regarding the company's Purpose Statement and Core Principles, rewarding the department whose members score the highest.

79. Provide practical internship and project opportunities for students, young pastors and seminarians in need of experience and short-term income.

80. Offer local in-home lodging for visiting missionaries and traveling ministry workers.

81. Give generously (i.e. tithe or more) based on company earnings, to worthy transformational projects in the community.

82. Encourage key executives to volunteer in a leadership/oversight capacity for a least one local benevolent Christian outreach/service organization.

83. Provide company speakers/testimonials for local Kingdom and community events.

84. Host monthly "birthday parties" for all employees born that month with a focus on thanksgiving, prayer, recognition and relationship building.

85. Mentor local start-up businesses and would-be entrepreneurs using company resources, talent and perhaps C12 materials.

86. Use the company's physical campus and web site to deliver clear Christ-centered messages.

87. Offer volunteer-led optional discipleship training using the company's Christian resource library.

88. Actively solicit and refer prospective employees who resonate with your firm's distinctive passion and vision. Develop synergistic relationships with one or more like-minded local staffing firms and colleges.

89. Sponsor missionary or service retreats for groups of employees who desire to minister as ambassadors for both Christ and your firm.

90. Release employees to engage in active ministry by systematically organizing, encouraging and celebrating such activity. Track and publicize ministry projects internally and budget support monies for each ministry ream/captain.

91. Provide a company prayer bulletin board(s) or a web utility.

92. Actively encourage all team members to brainstorm and critique company activities and methods against stated Biblical core principles.

93. Provide opportunities for extended short-term leaves without pay for personal mission/Kingdom service opportunities consistent with company values.

94. Maintain a private counseling/devotional room with appropriate support materials, set aside for discipling prayer and mentoring purposes.

95. Provide godly mentoring and tutoring for local school children.

96. Take time to clearly underscore and celebrate specific examples of decisions made to avoid moral compromises and confusion. Highlight stories and case studies where company employees dealt with difficult situations well, speaking the truth in love and acting sacrificially.

97. Have an annual employee/supplier/customer "open house" to display and celebrate company Christian values and principles, share supportive stories from staff members and recognize those who have exhibited what you promote.

98. Maintain the cleanest, safest, most excellent work environment in your industry and routinely celebrate those areas/teams who "lead the way".

99. Surprise your staff members, suppliers and customers with occasional "appreciation" gift baskets which include a well-crafted card expressing how your relationship reflects the Lord's provision and glory.

100. Sponsor youth athletic teams with uniforms and coaching that clearly promote Christian values. Make a big deal of it at season's end with a wonderful celebratory banquet.

101. Place evangelistic 'self-service' displays with literature and posted follow-up options in lobbies, vending areas and gathering spots.

Action Steps & Personal Accountability

From the list, select the three most accessible steps from Appendix C – Brainstorming the Possibilities. Rank by ease of application. Put the easiest to apply first, the next, second, etc. Keep the remainder of the list and arrange it in order of ease and readiness. As the first three items are implemented or completed take the next from your list and implement it and so on. Assign a person or committee to be accountable for coordinating the process, recording results and holding regular meetings to review and discuss progress. This might be done monthly or quarterly.

Idea: Implementation
Date

1. _____ _____
We expect to see the following results within one year:

_____

_____

_____

_____

2. _____ _____
We expect to see the following results within one year:

_____

_____

_____

_____

3. _____ _____
We expect to see the following results within one year:

_____

_____

_____

_____

Initial and sign below and have someone you respect (who will not be afraid to hold you accountable) sign as witness. Provide them with a copy of this page.

Initial:

_____ I will review results monthly or quarterly and make adjustments as needed.

_____ I will look at implementing other ideas from the list in _____ months.

In making this Action Plan, it is my intention to implement these and other actions to see my company used to share the Gospel of Jesus Christ in the unique portion of the marketplace that we serve.

Signed _____ Date_____

Witness _____ Date_____

I request the person who signed the sheet as a witness to call me in three months, six months, nine months and one year to discuss what results have occurred.

Signed _____ Date_____

Call me at_____ Date_____

A Formula for Fueling Ministry HyperGrowth

How pleased are you with the results of the ministry accomplished through your company to-date? Honestly, without either false humility or pride, how have you done? In relation to whatever the potential for ministry in your company might be, how are you doing?

For most of us the answers to the above questions are vexing, difficult and, for many (if not all) of us, convicting and a bit embarrassing.

I've had the privilege of having countless conversations and meetings with C12 members and other Christian business owners and CEOs over the past 25 years. There have been precious few that have been ecstatic, or even truly pleased, about the results they have achieved in realizing the potential for ministry through the business they run for God.

This phenomenon stands in stark contrast with a good number of similar conversations regarding results in the secular or worldly dimension of business such as sales, profits, and valuations. There have been many who have prospered so greatly in the world's measures of success that they have expressed wonder, amazement and humility. Not everyone of course, but many.

The sadness of this is the obvious reversal in ultimate importance of these two dimensions in terms of value to the individual reporting them, to the Body of Christ, and to God Himself. It takes only a brief moment of reflection to realize this truth and to become convicted. We all know that, in eternal terms, the ministry dimension, and the fruit of our work therein, is stunningly more important to us than business measures no matter how good the business metrics might be.

Just saying these things raises the question of where results come from. If our business grows faster in the less important dimension, that which is temporary and not eternal, and which will at some point become meaningless, can it really be God who is behind them even if the efforts and concentration that result in this growth diminish the commitment of similar effort and concentration on ministry which produces eternal results? The answer to this question may haunt some of us, but it is a sure thing that God does not work against Himself or put roadblocks in our way. Anything that diminishes the work of God does not come from God, but from the evil one.

Of course God can and does cause businesses to grow and to prosper in material terms. But when *He* does it's always as a means to greater ministry and never the cause for ministry diminution. Satan retains delegated control over much of the world's material goods and God allows him to use them to distract or confuse us. If material growth or prosperity takes us away from effective ministry they do not come as blessings from God, but as a curse from the pit of hell.

One day, during the next 20 to 50 years, everyone who reads these words will know this truth. There will be great benefit to those who accept and act on them today, and immeasurable loss to those who don't.

The clock ticks inexorably. Time and our opportunity are passing, day-by-day, hour-by-hour, moment-by-moment. Most of us have already squandered and wasted enough opportunity to be ashamed of ourselves before God. Is there anything that we might do to change the patterns we have been bound to and reverse the trends of apathy or ineffectiveness we have experienced?

If Nothing Changes, Nothing Changes

Yes there is a way. In Christ there is always a way as long as there is life and breath. We can change and reverse our experience. We can be set free from addictions and bad habits. We can have our relationships mended and restored. We are forgiven the moment we ask, and we have God's power within us to resist the lies and distractions of the evil one. The potential is there. The key that unlocks it is our willingness to change. If we are not willing to change and to make changes in the ways we have been doing the things we do, our future lives will merely be reflections of our past. "If nothing changes, nothing changes." If we would see hypergrowth in the ministry dimension of our business life experience, or in any other part of our lives for that matter, we must be willing to make changes. To the degree we are willing to change our thoughts and actions in faithful reliance on Him, we can expect differences in our results.

Our segment today is for those of us who know very well that we have not been all God would have us to be in fulfilling His call on our lives as Ambassadors for Christ to our business and industry, and are willing, even anxious to change. To those not so inclined, this will simply be some more good information.

If you are one of the former, the following is for you.

A Formula for Ministry HyperGrowth

1. The formula begins with the leader, you and me. Hypergrowth won't just happen, it must be led. Our first step will be taken in the area of daily devotional or quiet time. If you would see ministry hypergrowth in your company and life, the first step is to commit the first 60-90 minutes of every day to spending time with God. This step is non-negotiable. No Christian will ever gain the potential of his/her life in God without this discipline. We fool ourselves and cheapen the testimony of every great Christian by denying this simple truth and trying to find some easier route. There is none. If you choose to argue the point it simply shows you are not ready to change and, until you are, you will never see hypergrowth in ministry in your business or in your life. For at least the first three to five years, practice the following discipline during your quiet time:

   - Spend the first 30 minutes in Bible reading and study. Always read at least one chapter from the gospels during this time. Never allow yourself to be out from under the sound of Jesus' voice as He caused it to be recorded in His Word.
   - Next, spend 15 minutes in study of marketplace ministry related materials. A list of highly recommended resources are listed in C12's *Solid Foundation*.

- Devote the next 15 minutes to prayer. Following a time of adoration, confession and thanksgiving, pray for your own sanctification in your roles as child of God, spouse, parent. Before you begin to focus on the primary ministry in your life, pray for the other, higher priorities. Ask God to anoint you as son, spouse, and parent, and then as servant.

- Pray for God's direction in your ministry through business, for the team of co-laborers God has or will provide, for your lost employees, customers, suppliers, and competitors, and every day pray for God to use you AND your company in His work to further His Kingdom. This last portion is critical! Always pray to be used by God. Submit to Him anything that hinders His work through you and your business. Ask Him to let His life flow through you and your co-workers THIS day, everyday. 15 minutes of prayer may not seem like a lot, and it may grow and extend over time, but 15 minutes a day, every day, will make changes in your company that you can't believe. If you are married, encourage your spouse to join you in this discipline if possible. It will more than double the blessings from this commitment to prayer for both of you.

- Finally, your quiet time will be hugely enhanced if you keep a journal. Simply record your thoughts, questions for God, and thanks for His grace and answers to prayer. This should take 5 to 15 minutes. This journal is between you and Him. Writing intensifies our understanding and also gives us a helpful historical record to appreciate God's faithfulness.

Your daily quiet time with the Lord will be the foundation from which hypergrowth will spring. You must guard it as a sacred time to which all other commitments must yield! It cannot be seen as an option or it will fail. If God is first in your life, prove it by making Him first in every day.

2. Take your devotional time with you to work. The next step is to identify the co-laborers that God has provided to work with you as ministers in the business. If you don't already know who they are, make identifying them a part of your prayer time at home and ask God to lead you to them, and them to you.

Find out who they are and what their gifts and callings are. Why has God strategically sent them to you? How can they best be used to further the Kingdom? Get a sense for the team He has sovereignly assembled. Remember, ministry to and through the business is a corporate potential, not limited to only you.

3. Start each day with 15 minutes of prayer with your co-laborers. This may be before the official work day starts, or on company time, depending on your individual circumstance and conviction.

Spend the first half of the time giving thanks to God for the ministry He did through you yesterday. Name it and give thanks.

Spend the second half praying for the day just beginning. Pray for scheduled events and activities, that somehow ministry will flow through them. Don't ignore seemingly mundane things like meetings or telephone calls. EVERY DAY ask God to use you that day! Make this petition a certain part of every day's prayer. Don't let it become routine. The practice of thanking Him for the past day's ministry will help you here.

Keep it fresh! Look for His answers and give thanks when you see them. Ask Him for a harvest of fruit! Ask Him for souls! It's His will, pray in it!

Be disciplined in keeping the time to 15 minutes. Start and end on time.

4. Have a three-day retreat with your team each year. If you have to, pay for it with your own money. Don't let the fact that some other employees won't or can't participate stop you. Depending on your individual circumstances you may need to do this as an unofficial function done on a purely personal basis. It isn't "optional" in the sense that anyone who doesn't want to participate isn't really a part of this team in the first place.

Don't be intimidated! Hypergrowth is not for wimps! Instead be creative, draw the people God has given you apart for a time of prayer and planning. Include recreation and worship, but the primary purpose of this time is to do three things:

- To make a ministry plan for the next twelve months.
- To establish a system of metrics and record-keeping to capture and evaluate ministry results.
- After the first year, review results and make needed changes to the plan. If you need help to do these things, bring in a facilitator.

5. Each quarter, go off-site for a half day of prayer, review, and renewal. Deal with current relational issues that may have come up within the team. Make unity a priority.

Don't be deceived. If you are following a path of hypergrowth in ministry, you and the team will be engaged in spiritual warfare, big-time! One of the enemy's most successful weapons is to sow discord, jealousy, and strife among well-meaning, but unaware believers. He has been very successful in using the curse of busyness in Christian companies to screen us from seeing and sensing the potential divisions and misunderstandings that he uses to hinder us.

Everything he has used to derail a great church will be used against you as you pursue God's plan for your business. You and your staff of believers will be tempted in all the same ways. Sex sin, materialism, and pride will come against you. Lies about one another will be whispered in your ears. Expect it. But don't be put off by it. Greater is He that is in you than he that is in the world, but you must give Him time and opportunity to work. Walk in The Light together. If you do, you will have true fellowship, and the blood of Christ will cleanse you from all unrighteousness.

6. End every day with a clean slate before God. Finish each day in prayer. Use this end-of-the-day prayer time to confess sin and seek forgiveness, to pray for personal and family needs, and for the other needs and ministries God lays on your heart. Again, if you are married, and it is possible, including your spouse in this practice will multiply the value exponentially. Try to make God's Word the last thing you allow to enter your mind before you fall asleep.

Getting Started

Obviously, there are other components that will fill in the cracks around these basics. God will lead and develop in His personal and creative way as we seek abounding fruit in His service. This formula is not meant to be exhaustive or legalistic. If you have a better way, pursue it. But this formula WILL work, and will produce hypergrowth ministry results, if you are willing to make the changes it requires, whatever they are.

For some of us the changes will not be so great, seeming more like adjustments and increased emphasis. For others the things outlined above will seem overwhelming, nearly impossible. Well, to those having that reaction, be assured, they are not. They represent only a small investment of time and effort in comparison to our overall work effort. It would be a very sad thing indeed if any Christian would be found unwilling to do for God what he would be very willing to do for money. Think about it. What if the previously outlined recommendations were to have been presented as a plan which guarantees that follow-through would make one a mega-millionaire? Would it be hard to find the commitment if that were so? Well, the payoff for this effort is so much greater. The treasures that will be laid-up in heaven, by those who follow it, will be worth far more to them than all of the millions that the world might offer. They will last and have great value forever. No, it's not too much to ask. In fact, it's not really enough, but it will certainly make a good start!

C12 GUIDING PRINCIPLES

MISSION To change the world by bringing forth the Kingdom of God in the marketplace through the companies and lives of those He calls to run businesses for Him.

VISION To see an active global Christian CEO/Owner network with C12 groups in every community of 50,000 or more.

DOCTRINE Simply, Jesus Christ is Lord, the whole Bible is wholly true, God has an eternal plan for each believer's life and that plan includes their business.

PROMISE To be an example of all we promote and to be accountable to our members seeking their correction when any deviation may appear. We serve as a resource for education, encouragement, challenge, inspiration, and accountability.

C12 groups meet monthly across America and are impacting business owners, their employees, customers, suppliers, and competitors for Christ. Christian business owners and CEOs are learning the significance of leading thriving companies as platforms for ministry, and discovering eternal as well as temporal benefits, as they "build great businesses for a greater purpose."

If you are a Christian business Owner or CEO and are interested in learning more about becoming a C12 member, or possibly starting a group in your area, please visit our website or contact us directly.

The C12 Group, LLC
4101 Piedmont Parkway
Greensboro, NC 27410
336-841-7100
www.C12Group.com